teeny tiny talks

volume four

I Am a Child of God

teeny tiny talks

volume four

I Am a Child of God

Written by Kimiko Christensen Hammari
Illustrated by Crystal Myers

CFI
Springville, Utah

ISBN 13: 978-1-59955-109-8

Published by CFI, an imprint of Cedar Fort, Inc., 2373 W. 700 S., Springville, UT, 84663
Distributed by Cedar Fort, Inc. www.cedarfort.com

Cover design by Nicole Williams
Cover design © 2007 by Lyle Mortimer
Cover illustration by Glenn Harmon
Edited by Annaliese B. Cox

Printed in the United States of America

10 9 8 7 6 5 4 3 2 1

Printed on acid-free paper

table of contents

january theme

I am a child of God, and He has a plan for me.

("Proclamation," paragraph 2)

talk one

I learned of and accepted Heavenly Father's plan. I have a divine destiny.

In the premortal life I lived with God
And learned of His great plan
To test and try our faith in Him
By creating Earth and man.

I cried for joy at this great plan
And the chance to come to earth.
I learned and grew and did all I could
To prepare for my earthly birth.

For I knew that God had a plan for me—
He called it divine destiny—
Where I could become perfect just like Him
And live in glory eternally.

In the premortal life I lived with God
And learned of His great plan
To test and try our faith in Him
By creating Earth and man.

I cried for joy at this great plan
And the chance to come to earth.
I learned and grew and did all I could
To prepare for my earthly birth.

For I knew that God had a plan for me—
He called it divine destiny—
Where I could become perfect just like Him
And live in glory eternally.

talk two

Heavenly Father gave me agency. I chose to follow His plan.

Heavenly Father gave us a special gift—
A gift called agency.
That means we choose all by ourselves
Whether to be captive or be free.

Because I had my agency,
I chose to follow Christ.
I chose to come down to this earth
And partake of His great sacrifice.

I'm grateful I can be part of God's plan
And choose to follow Him.
I want to build His kingdom on earth
And be free from evil and sin.

Heavenly Father gave us a special gift—
A gift called agency.
That means we choose all by ourselves
Whether to be captive or be free.

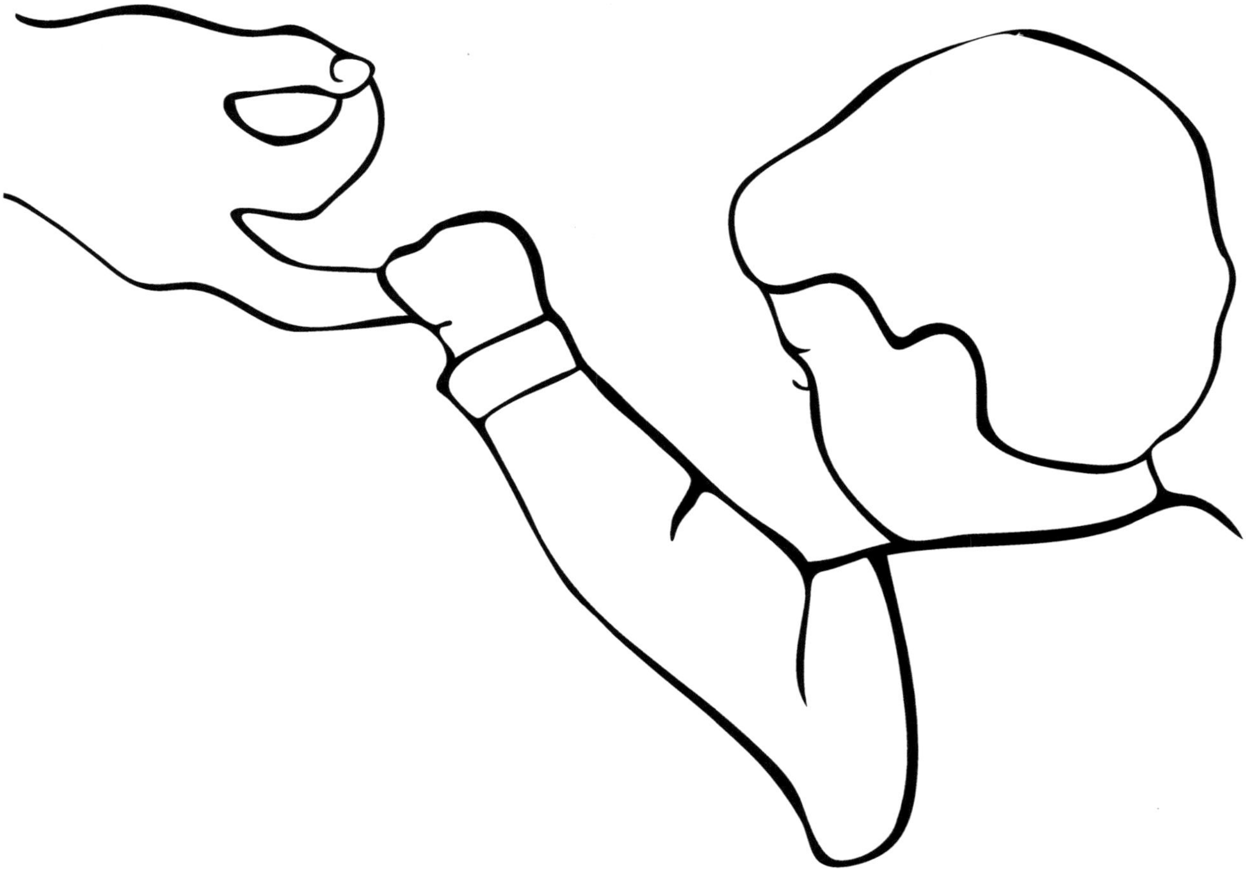

Because I had my agency,
I chose to follow Christ.
I chose to come down to this earth
And partake of His great sacrifice.

The Plan of Salvation

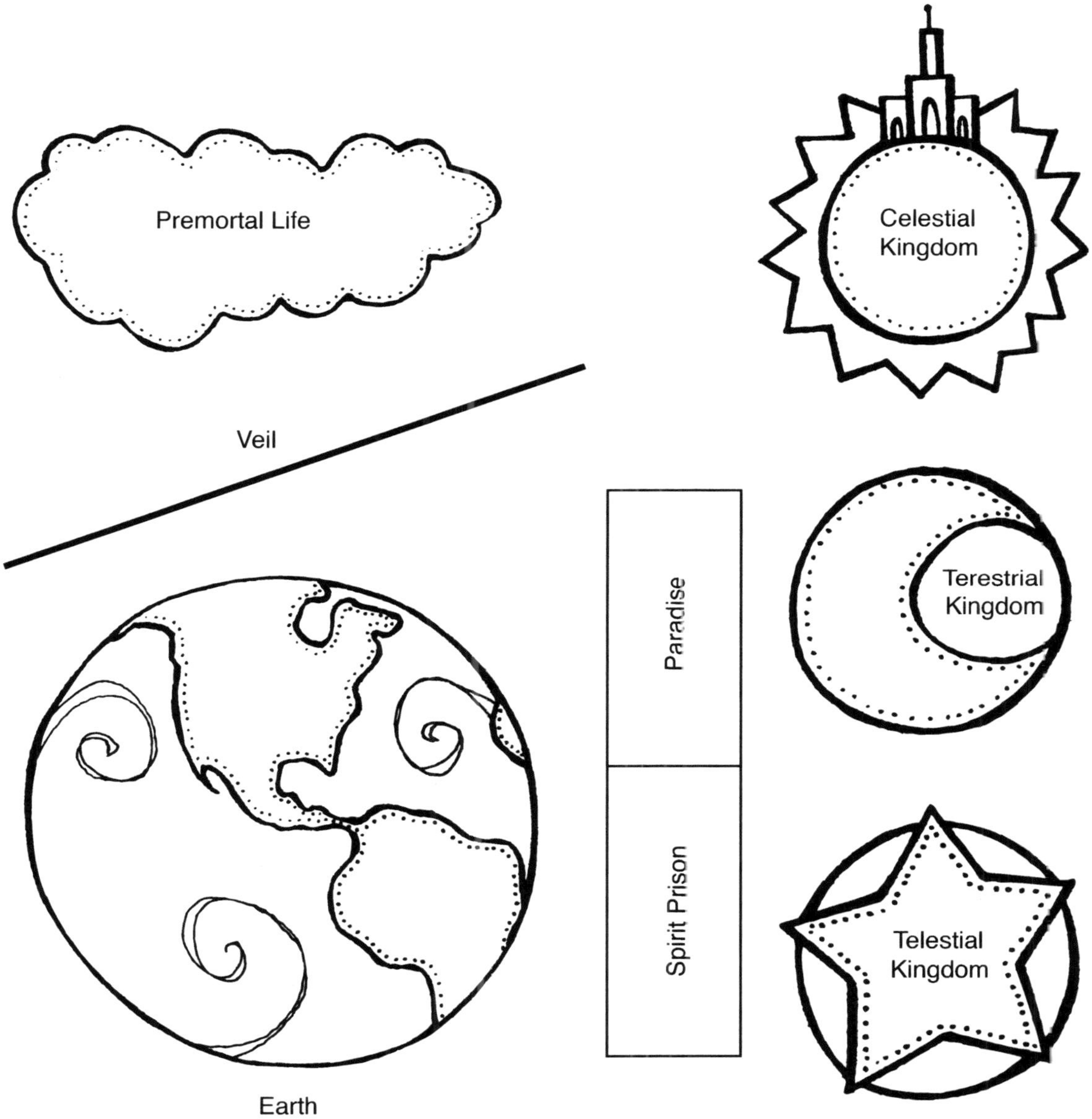

I'm grateful I can be part of God's plan
And choose to follow Him.
I want to build His kingdom on earth
And be free from evil and sin.

february theme

The scriptures teach me about Heavenly Father and Jesus Christ and how to return to Them.

(2 Nephi 4:15)

talk one

Bible stories teach me how to live the gospel.

I love to read of Moses,
Who parted the Red Sea
So that the children of Israel
Could finally be free.

I love to read of Abraham
And his love for Jesus Christ,
And how he was willing to offer
His son as a sacrifice.

The prophets in the Bible
Help me choose the right.
They show me how to live my life
And see the truth and light.

I love to read of Moses,
Who parted the Red Sea
So that the children of Israel
Could finally be free.

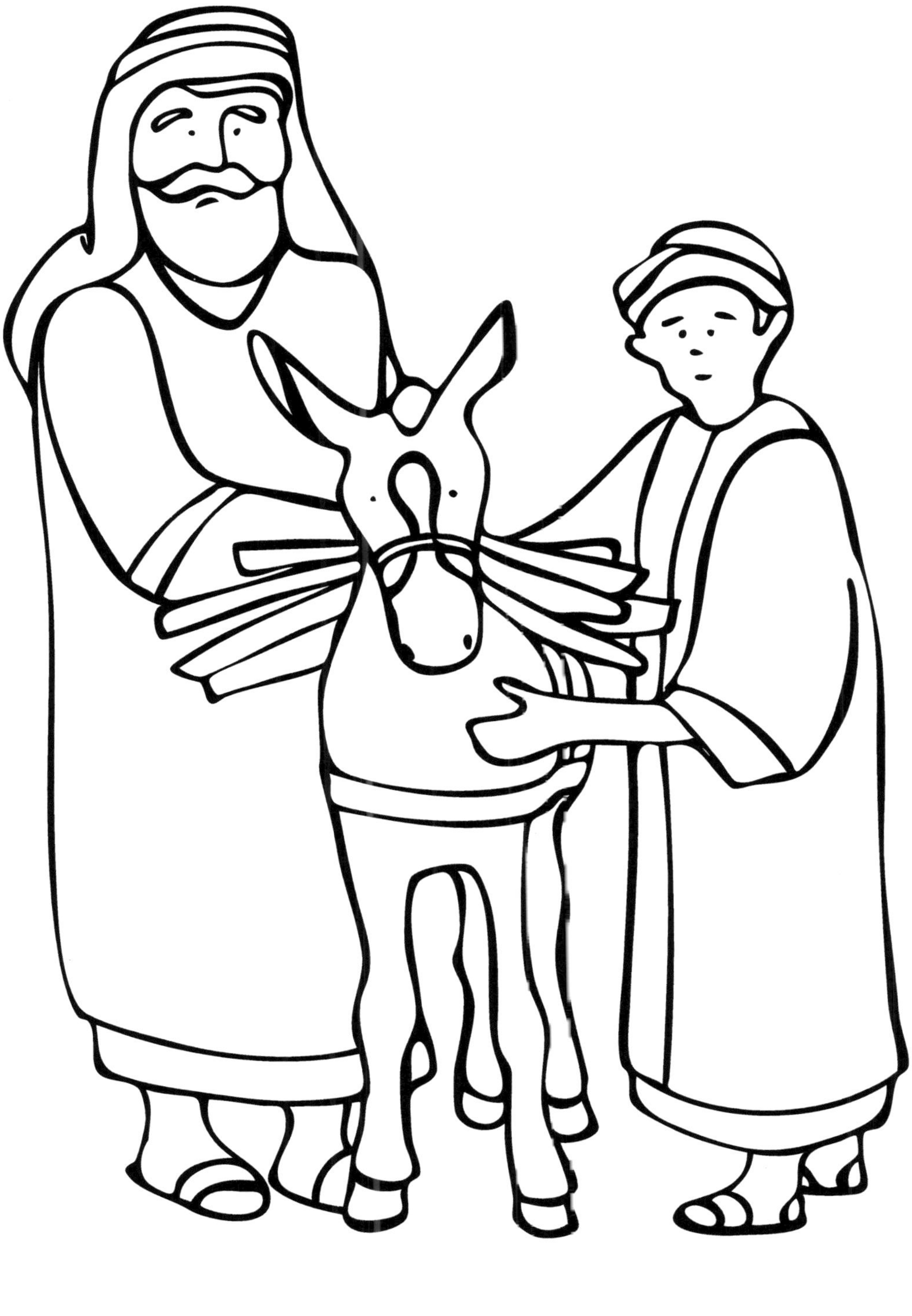

I love to read of Abraham
And his love for Jesus Christ,
And how he was willing to offer
His son as a sacrifice.

The prophets in the Bible
Help me choose the right.
They show me how to live my life
And see the truth and light.

talk two

Book of Mormon stories teach me how to live the gospel.

Lehi and his family
Left Jerusalem
Because the Lord had warned them
Of great destruction that would come.

They traveled in the wilderness
And then across the seas
So they could reach the promised land
And worship as they pleased.

Book of Mormon stories
Show me how to follow God
And how to hold on firmly
To the precious iron rod.

Lehi and his family
Left Jerusalem
Because the Lord had warned them
Of great destruction that would come.

They traveled in the wilderness
And then across the seas
So they could reach the promised land
And worship as they pleased.

Book of Mormon stories
Show me how to follow God
And how to hold on firmly
To the precious iron rod.

march theme

Jesus is my Savior.

(1 John 4:14)

talk one

Jesus Christ showed me how to do the will of Heavenly Father.

In the Garden of Gethsemane
Jesus prayed to God above
And asked if there was another way
To show mankind His love.

But Jesus knew what He must do—
He must perform the dreadful task.
He must bear the burdens of the world
And do all His Father asked.

And so our Savior died for us
To do the Father's will.
He gave His life to give us life
And all righteousness fulfill.

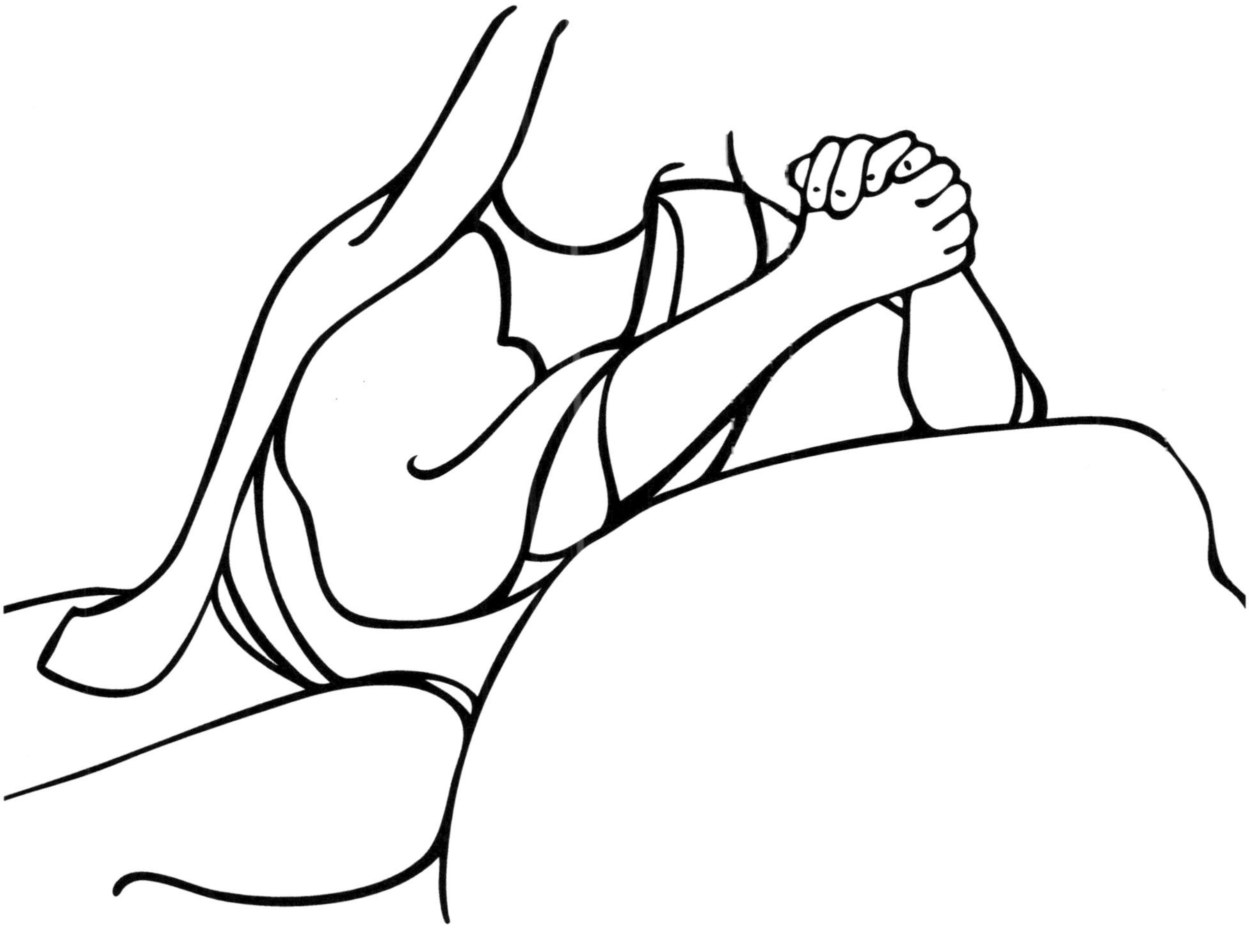

In the Garden of Gethsemane
Jesus prayed to God above
And asked if there was another way
To show mankind His love.

But Jesus knew what He must do—
He must perform the dreadful task.
He must bear the burdens of the world
And do all His Father asked.

And so our Savior died for us
To do the Father's will.
He gave His life to give us life
And all righteousness fulfill.

talk two

Jesus Christ lives today. He will come again.

That Easter morn' the tomb was bare
Where Jesus had been lain.
The Savior rose on the third day
And conquered death and pain.

He brought new life to all mankind
And taught a precious truth—
All of us will live again.
His nail prints stand as proof.

Someday Christ will come again
And teach us face to face.
I cannot wait to be with Him
And feel His loving grace.

That Easter morn' the tomb was bare
Where Jesus had been lain.
The Savior rose on the third day
And conquered death and pain.

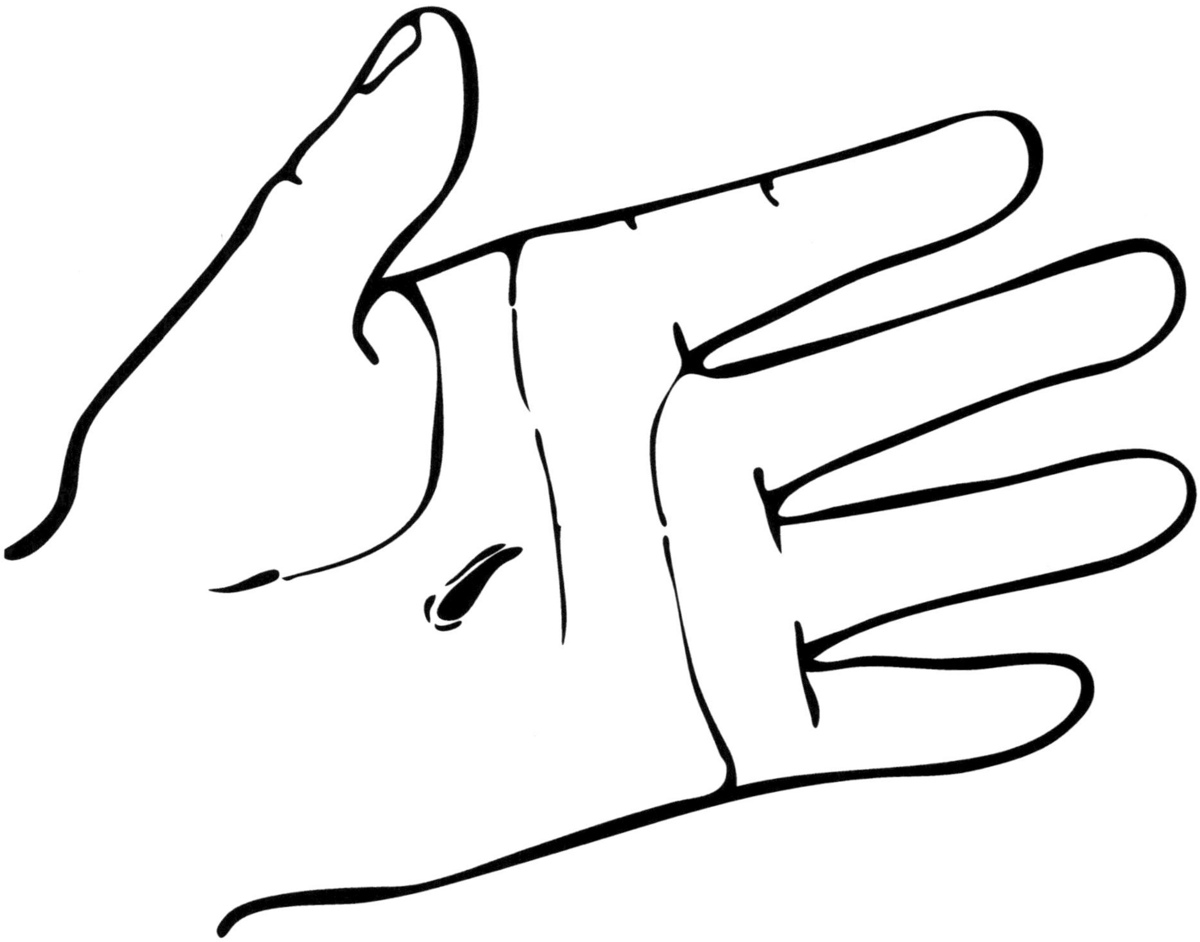

He brought new life to all mankind
And taught a precious truth—
All of us will live again.
His nail prints stand as proof.

Someday Christ will come again
And teach us face to face.
I cannot wait to be with Him
And feel His loving grace.

april theme

The prophet teaches me that I should love and forgive others.

(Amos 3:7)

talk one

The prophet teaches me that I should love and forgive others.

Sometimes people do things
That make us really sad,
And we are often tempted
To think that they are bad.

But the prophet teaches different—
We must show our love to others
By forgiving them of all their wrongs
Because they are our brothers.

I feel good when I forgive;
It makes the burden leave.
I feel peace within my heart
Because my soul is free.

Sometimes people do things
That make us really sad,
And we are often tempted
To think that they are bad.

But the prophet teaches different—
We must show our love to others
By forgiving them of all their wrongs
Because they are our brothers.

I feel good when I forgive;
It makes the burden leave.
I feel peace within my heart
Because my soul is free.

talk two

The prophet teaches me what I must do to live with God again.

Sometimes I am confused
And don't know right from wrong,
But often my confusion
Doesn't last for very long.

Because all I have to do
Is learn what the prophet taught.
Then I'll know the will of God
And do what I know I ought.

The prophet is inspired
To teach us how to live our lives
So we can keep our covenants
And return to God and Jesus Christ.

Sometimes I am confused
And don't know right from wrong,
But often my confusion
Doesn't last for very long.

Because all I have to do
Is learn what the prophet taught.
Then I'll know the will of God
And do what I know I ought.

The prophet is inspired
To teach us how to live our lives
So we can keep our covenants
And return to God and Jesus Christ.

may theme

Heavenly Father planned for me to come to a family.
I can strengthen my family now.

("Proclamation," paragraph 1)

talk one

Each member of my family has a divine role.

I'm blessed to have a family
That helps me choose the right,
That loves the Lord and does His will
And knows the purpose of this life.

Each member of my family
Has a divine role
To build God's kingdom here on earth
And share the gospel with each soul.

I'm thankful for my family.
I'll help in every way I can
To help them learn of Jesus Christ
And follow God's great plan.

I'm blessed to have a family
That helps me choose the right,
That loves the Lord and does His will
And knows the purpose of this life.

Each member of my family
Has a divine role
To build God's kingdom here on earth
And share the gospel with each soul.

I'm thankful for my family.
I'll help in every way I can
To help them learn of Jesus Christ
And follow God's great plan.

talk two

The priesthood can bless and strengthen my family.

The priesthood is the power
To act in Jesus' name,
To heal the sick and bless the weak,
To heal the crippled and the lame.

Through the blessings of the priesthood
I can receive an ordinance
So I can grow and be like God
And keep my covenants.

I'm grateful that my father
Brings the priesthood in my home
So I can know of God's great love
Through the miracles I'm shown.

The priesthood is the power
To act in Jesus' name,
To heal the sick and bless the weak,
To heal the crippled and the lame.

Through the blessings of the priesthood
I can receive an ordinance
So I can grow and be like God
And keep my covenants.

I'm grateful that my father
Brings the priesthood in my home
So I can know of God's great love
Through the miracles I'm shown.

june theme

The temple is a blessing for me and my family.

(D&C 124:40)

talk one

My tithing helps to build temples.

Each time I earn a dollar
I set aside a dime
To give to God as tithing
Because I know it isn't mine.

But giving up the money
Has never made me poor
Because a portion of my tithing
Builds temples for the Lord.

The blessings of the temple
Are worth much more than gold.
They seal us to our family—
A gift that can't be sold.

Each time I earn a dollar
I set aside a dime
To give to God as tithing
Because I know it isn't mine.

But giving up the money
Has never made me poor
Because a portion of my tithing
Builds temples for the Lord.

The blessings of the temple
Are worth much more than gold.
They seal us to our family—
A gift that can't be sold.

talk two

I will do family history work so my ancestors can receive temple blessings.

I have family in the spirit world
Who never got baptized
Because they didn't learn about the gospel
Or the Church of Jesus Christ.

But the temple makes it possible
For them to have a second chance.
They can be baptized and sealed
And receive each ordinance.

I will do my family history
To help my ancestors
Receive the blessings of the temple
And live forever with the Lord.

I have family in the spirit world
Who never got baptized
Because they didn't learn about the gospel
Or the Church of Jesus Christ.

But the temple makes it possible
For them to have a second chance.
They can be baptized and sealed
And receive each ordinance.

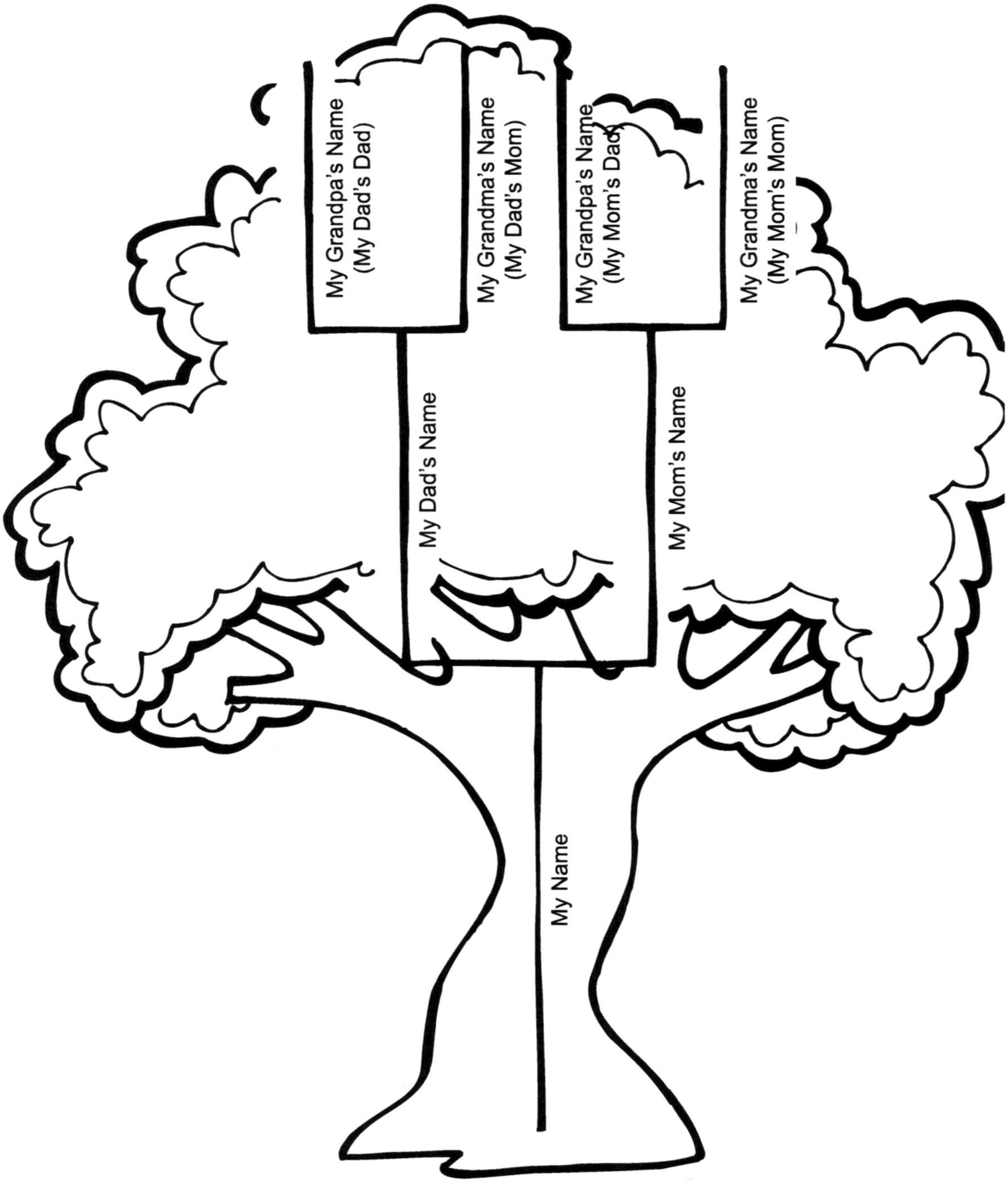

I will do my family history
To help my ancestors
Receive the blessings of the temple
And live forever with the Lord.

july theme

Because I know we are all children of God,
I will share the gospel with others.

(D&C 18:15)

talk one

I will prepare to be a missionary by being faithful and obedient.

I can't wait to serve a mission.
I want to go today
To share the Book of Mormon
And teach others how to pray.

But first I must prepare
And learn to pray myself.
I must study all the scriptures
And learn of their great wealth.

And then when I am ready,
I'll receive that sacred call.
I'll learn to love the people
And share the gospel with them all.

I can't wait to serve a mission.
I want to go today
To share the Book of Mormon
And teach others how to pray.

But first I must prepare
And learn to pray myself.
I must study all the scriptures
And learn of their great wealth.

And then when I am ready,
I'll receive that sacred call.
I'll learn to love the people
And share the gospel with them all.

talk two

Living the gospel standards helps me to be a missionary now.

Although I'm still too young
To be a full-time missionary,
I can practice good traits now
And resist the adversary.

By living gospel standards
And doing what is right,
I share with others my beliefs
By the way I live my life.

I want to share the gospel.
I'll help others learn the truth
By making good decisions
While I am in my youth.

Although I'm still too young
To be a full-time missionary,
I can practice good traits now
And resist the adversary.

By living gospel standards
And doing what is right,
I share with others my beliefs
By the way I live my life.

I want to share the gospel.
I'll help others learn the truth
By making good decisions
While I am in my youth.

august theme

I will show my faith in Jesus Christ by being baptized and confirmed.

(D&C 68:27)

talk one

The Holy Ghost will prompt me to repent and live righteously after I am baptized and confirmed.

When I'm baptized I'll be so clean
And start a life brand new.
I'll promise Jesus Christ
To be pure in all I say and do.

But at times it will be hard
To make the proper choice.
And that's when I must listen
For the still, small voice.

When I'm confirmed, the Holy Ghost
Will come and dwell with me.
He'll teach me and He'll guide me
To live more righteously.

When I'm baptized I'll be so clean
And start a life brand new.
I'll promise Jesus Christ
To be pure in all I say and do.

But at times it will be hard
To make the proper choice.
And that's when I must listen
For the still, small voice.

When I'm confirmed, the Holy Ghost
Will come and dwell with me.
He'll teach me and He'll guide me
To live more righteously.

talk two

Heavenly Father forgives all who truly repent.

It's often hard to choose the right
And stay away from sin.
All of us will make mistakes
And feel a pain within.

But we don't have to stay that way.
God wants us to repent.
We can start again and be forgiven
If we have real intent.

Our Father will forgive us
And wash our sins away
So we can live a righteous life
And return to Him someday.

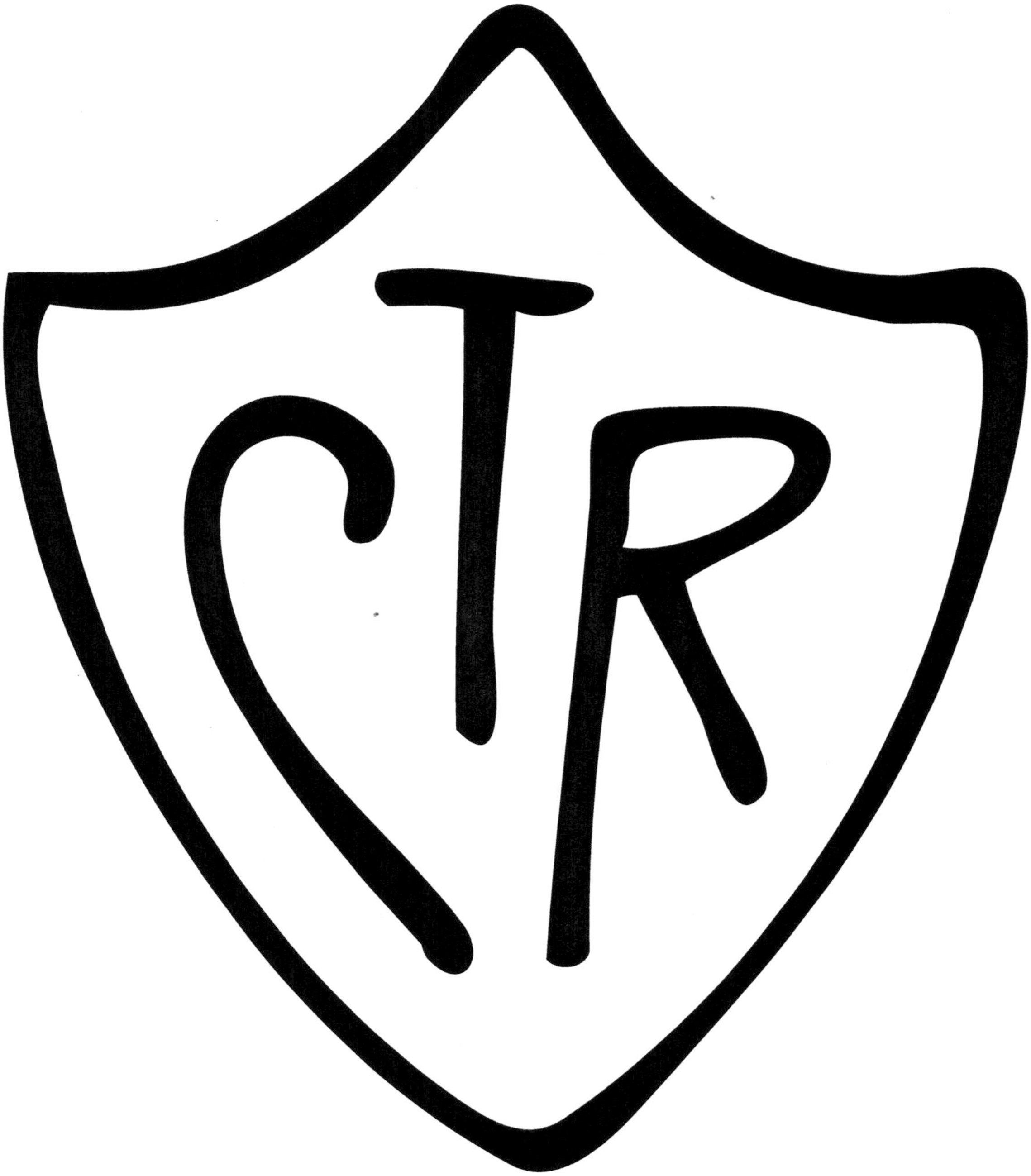

It's often hard to choose the right
And stay away from sin.
All of us will make mistakes
And feel a pain within.

But we don't have to stay that way.
God wants us to repent.
We can start again and be forgiven
If we have real intent.

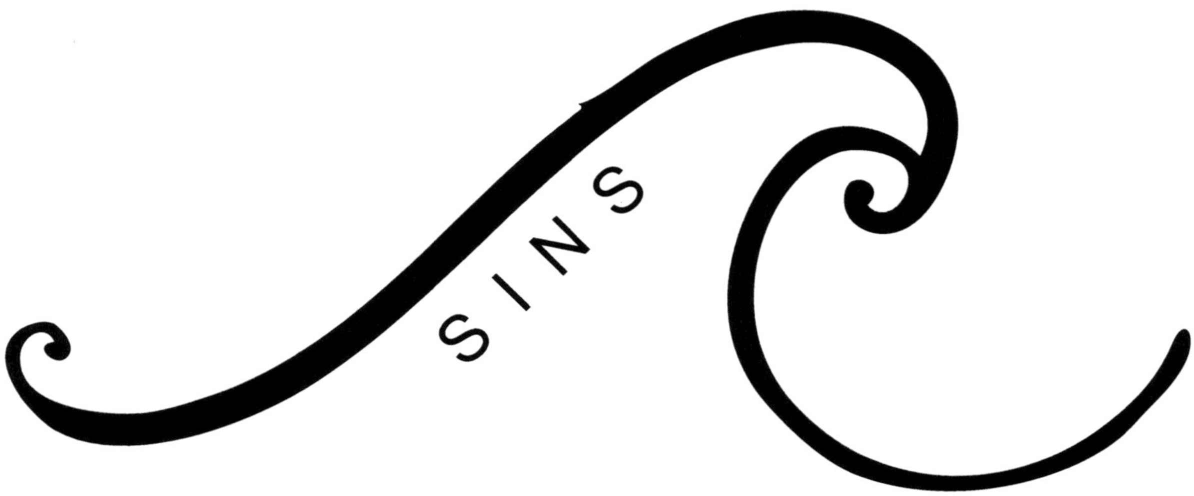

Our Father will forgive us
And wash our sins away
So we can live a righteous life
And return to Him someday.

september theme

I can pray to Heavenly Father, and He will hear and answer my prayers.

(Mark 11:24)

talk one

Heavenly Father wants me to pray to Him often—anytime, anywhere.

Heavenly Father loves me.
He wants to hear from me each day.
And so each morning and each night,
I kneel down and start to pray.

But sometimes I am not at home
When I feel like saying a prayer,
And that's when I remember,
I can do it anywhere!

Our Heavenly Father hears us
No matter where we are—
At home or school or church or play—
He's never very far.

Heavenly Father loves me.
He wants to hear from me each day.
And so each morning and each night,
I kneel down and start to pray.

But sometimes I am not at home
When I feel like saying a prayer,
And that's when I remember,
I can do it anywhere!

Our Heavenly Father hears us
No matter where we are—
At home or school or church or play—
He's never very far.

talk two

Heavenly Father knows me. He will answer my prayers in ways that are best for me.

Heavenly Father knows me
And always listens when I pray.
But because He knows what's best for me,
He'll sometimes answer "nay."

He cannot always give me
All that I request
Because sometimes what I want
May not be what is best.

But He will always give me
What will put me on the path
To have more faith in Jesus Christ
And receive all the Father hath.

Heavenly Father knows me
And always listens when I pray.
But because He knows what's best for me,
He'll sometimes answer "nay."

He cannot always give me
All that I request
Because sometimes what I want
May not be what is best.

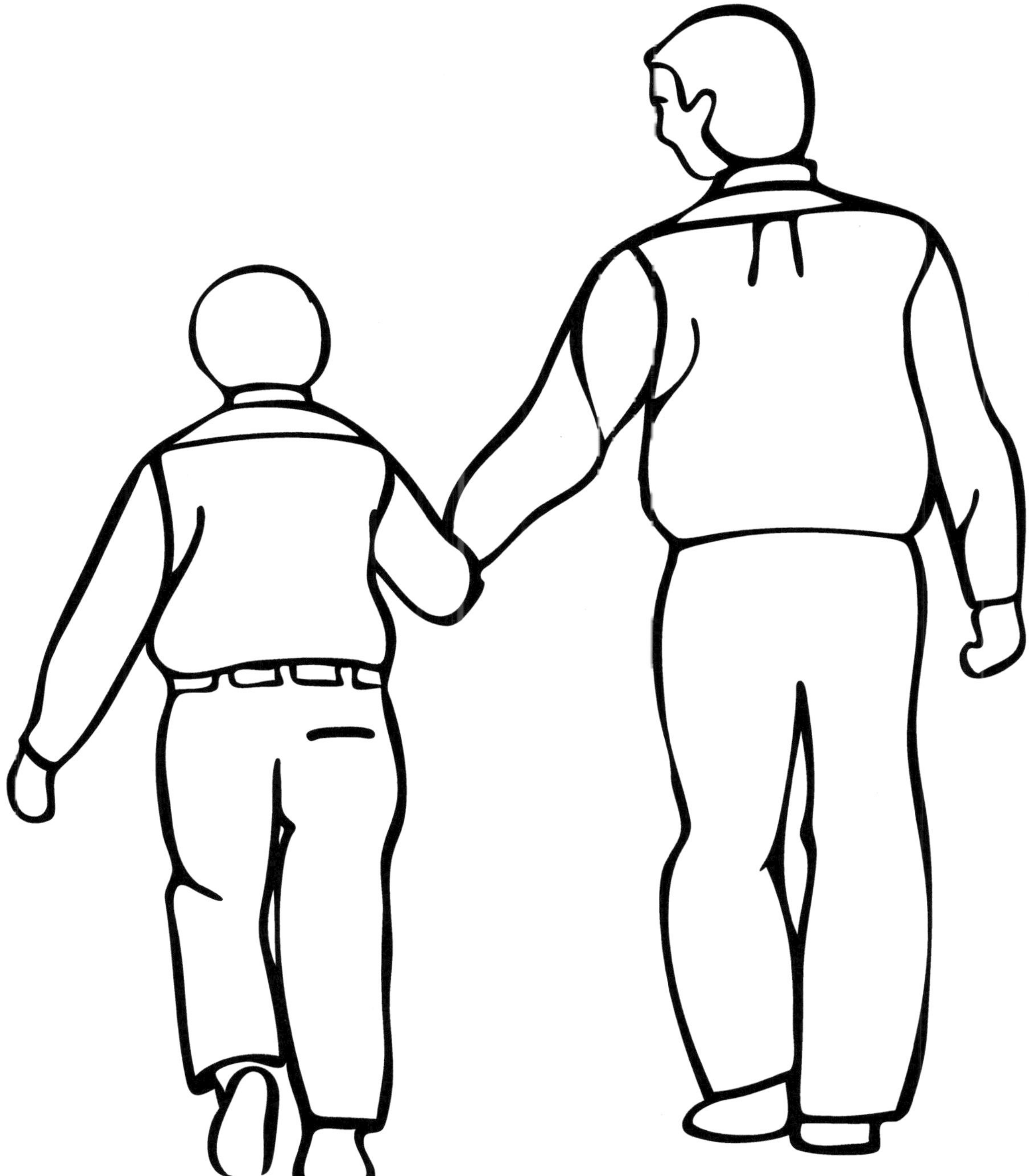

But He will always give me
What will put me on the path
To have more faith in Jesus Christ
And receive all the Fcther hath.

october theme

Because I am His child, I will serve God with all my heart, might, mind, and strength.

(D&C 4:2)

talk one

I can serve Heavenly Father by serving others.

There was a king named Benjamin
Who preached of charity
And taught us how to serve each other
For all eternity.

When you are in the service
Of your fellow man,
You're in the service of your God
And following His plan.

I want to serve my Father.
I'll start this very day
By serving those around me
In all I do and say.

There was a king named Benjamin
Who preached of charity
And taught us how to serve each other
For all eternity.

When you are in the service
Of your fellow man,
You're in the service of your God
And following His plan.

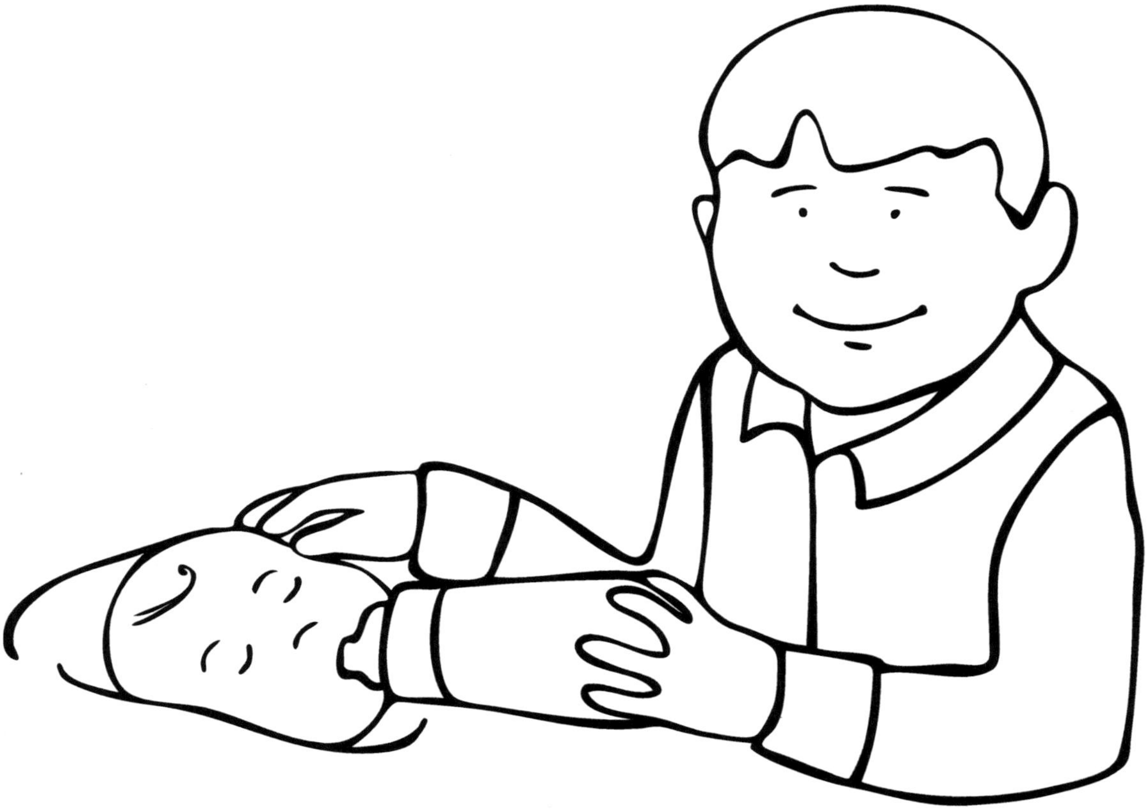

I want to serve my Father.
I'll start this very day
By serving those around me
In all I do and say.

talk two

Because others serve me, I too want to serve.

My brother helped me do my chores.
I felt so good inside.
He put a smile upon my face—
A grin so big and wide.

He helped me learn how service
Can really help another.
I'm grateful for this lesson
From my loving older brother.

I too will serve my fellow man
And in turn serve God above
So I can know our Savior
And feel His perfect love.

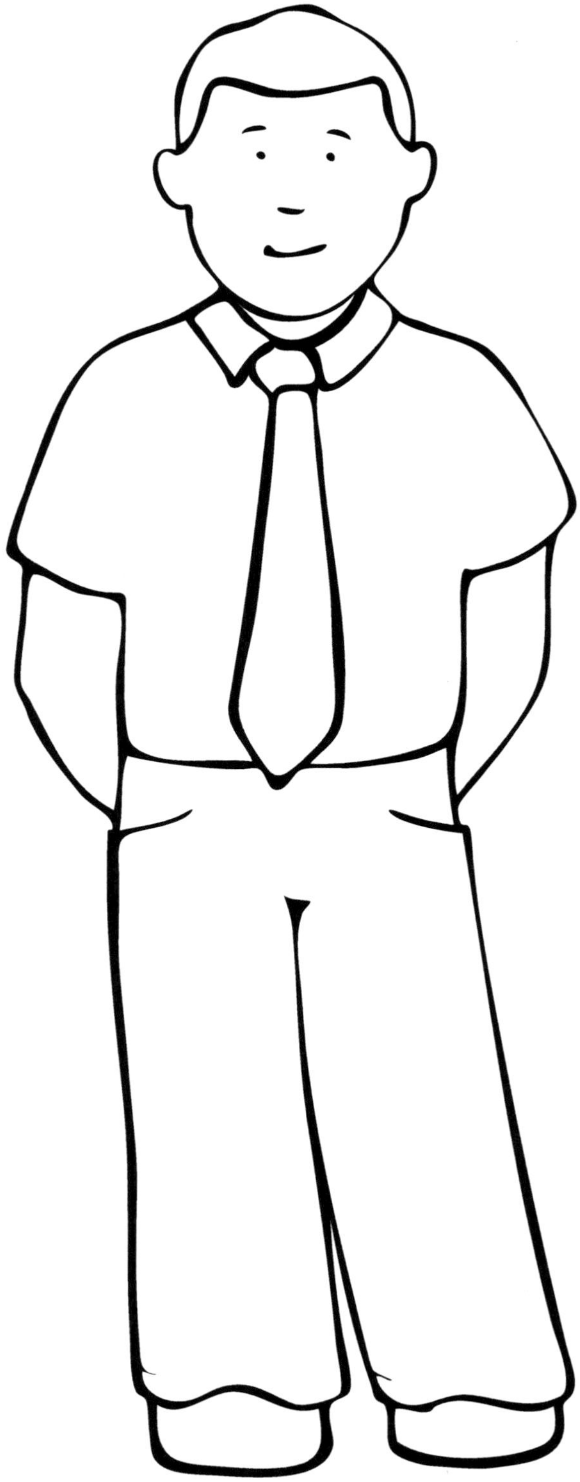

My brother helped me do my chores.
I felt so good inside.
He put a smile upon my face—
A grin so big and wide.

He helped me learn how service
Can really help another.
I'm grateful for this lesson
From my loving older brother.

I too will serve my fellow man
And in turn serve God above
So I can know our Savior
And feel His perfect love.

november theme

I am thankful to know that
we are all children of God.

(D&C 59:7)

talk one

I am thankful to be a beloved child of God.

I am a child of God.
I know this to be true
Because I feel Him near me
In everything I do.

I'm created in His image.
He made me who I am
And blessed me with my talents
To fulfill a special plan.

I'm thankful for this knowledge
The Spirit gives to me
So I can live a righteous life
And be with God eternally.

I am a child of God.
I know this to be true
Because I feel Him near me
In everything I do.

I'm created in His image.
He made me who I am
And blessed me with my talents
To fulfill a special plan.

I'm thankful for this knowledge
The Spirit gives to me
So I can live a righteous life
And be with God eternally.

talk two

Heavenly Father loves all His children.

Heavenly Father loves us.
There is nothing we can do
To take away the precious love
That He has for me and you.

It doesn't matter what we are—
If we're smart or rich or poor.
It doesn't matter if we're black or white—
Each day He loves us more.

I'm grateful that no matter what
Heavenly Father will be there
To listen to my daily prayers
And to show me that He cares.

Heavenly Father loves us.
There is nothing we can do
To take away the precious love
That He has for me and you.

It doesn't matter what we are—
If we're smart or rich or poor.
It doesn't matter if we're black or white—
Each day He loves us more.

I'm grateful that no matter what
Heavenly Father will be there
To listen to my daily prayers
And to show me that He cares.

december theme

I love my Savior, Jesus Christ, and His restored gospel

(2 Nephi 25:26)

talk one

The prophets foretold that Jesus Christ would come to the earth.

For many years the prophets taught
That Christ would come to earth.
They looked forward to that sacred day
And watched for signs of His birth.

They had great faith that He would come
To redeem us from the Fall.
He'd heal the sick and cure the blind
And give new life to all.

I'm grateful for my Savior.
I know He came to earth for me.
I'm grateful for His sacrifice
And love Him tenderly.

For many years the prophets taught
That Christ would come to earth.
They looked forward to that sacred day
And watched for signs of His birth.

They had great faith that He would come
To redeem us from the Fall.
He'd heal the sick and cure the blind
And give new life to all.

I'm grateful for my Savior.
I know He came to earth for me.
I'm grateful for His sacrifice
And love Him tenderly.

talk two

Jesus Christ restored His gospel through the Prophet Joseph Smith.

There was a time not long ago,
Called the Great Apostasy,
When Christ's true church was not on earth
And no one held the priesthood keys.

But Jesus Christ called Joseph Smith
To restore His ancient church
So all mankind could know the truth
And end their fruitless search.

I'm grateful for this prophet
Who had faith enough to pray
And ask our Heavenly Father
To show him the right way.

There was a time not long ago,
Called the Great Apostasy,
When Christ's true church was not on earth
And no one held the priesthood keys.

But Jesus Christ called Joseph Smith
To restore His ancient church
So all mankind could know the truth
And end their fruitless search.

I'm grateful for this prophet
Who had faith enough to pray
And ask our Heavenly Father
To show him the right way.

0 26575 71098 4